03-9786

MEMOIRS of a ROSE MAN
by J. Horace McFarland

MEMOIRS
of a
ROSE MAN

TALES FROM BREEZE HILL

by

J. HORACE McFARLAND

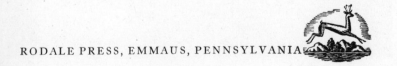

RODALE PRESS, EMMAUS, PENNSYLVANIA

*I*T WAS MY GOOD
fortune that J. Horace McFarland and I were
contemporaries and intimate associates. He
was a vigorous, constructive man, who built
up a large and influential business, was a sin-
cere lover of plants and gardens and a good
grower of them, responsive to beauty everywhere, lover of his fellow men, a cheerful
companion.

He was a man of positive opinions; often he
and I disagreed radically on some practice or
problem, but that never made any difference
in our close friendship, because he was direct
and religiously honest. As a rosarian his life
was outstanding.

I am glad that a memoir of his life and
work is to appear. It will keep his influence
alive. He stood for every good thing.

L. H. BAILEY
Director, Bailey Hortorium
N. Y. State College of Agriculture

Cornell University, Ithaca, N. Y.
November 10, 1948

INTRODUCTION

FEW other Americans, if any, have fostered the art of gardening with the earnestness and enthusiasm of Dr. J. Horace McFarland. We are fortunate in having the few vignettes of his special interests contained in this work.

On numerous occasions Dr. McFarland was urged to write an autobiography. Why he never did is understandable to his more intimate friends. His philosophy was to look forward, to build upon the past but not to reconstruct it. For him, each day was better than the one before and each tomorrow looked brighter than today.

Dr. McFarland was a man of exceedingly wide interests and he was a pioneer in many movements. No cause that promised to improve life in America was so minor as to escape his attention or too great for his energy and vision.

He was best known perhaps for his love of roses and his ability to inspire a love for them in others. But he was much more than a rosarian; indeed, even more than a horticulturist. Through the past seventy-five years there has hardly been an activity in the field of horticulture in which his influence has not been felt. For years he was an ardent worker for better civic planning, for state and national parks, and for the preservation of the beauty of Niagara Falls. He pioneered in plant photography, in horticultural printing, and he can be considered the father of the modern seed and nursery catalog. He encouraged the introduction of valuable plants, the development of new varieties and perhaps did more to popularize gardening as a recreation than any other man. Many special horticultural groups, besides the American Rose Society, claimed him as their chief apostle and he served them all with distinction.

But this book of memoirs is delightful, not

because it portrays the personal relationships of a distinguished man but because it emphasizes his simplicity, sincerity, and rich human qualities. Actually, *Memoirs of a Rose Man* is more concerned with his contemporaries than with Dr. McFarland himself; yet as he tells of his associations with others, his stature grows by his own humility. Even though his writings on gardening have been voluminous, none are quite as intimate as those found in this book. He answers the questions that I am sure have long been in the minds of his many admirers about his background and personal feelings.

As might be expected, the setting for most of the book is Breeze Hill. It is impossible to separate Dr. McFarland from his beloved Breeze Hill home. Certainly no other American garden is more widely known. It is neither large nor pretentious in terms of famous show places, but no private garden of today has provided more horticultural lore.

These memoirs will be cherished dearly by the countless friends who knew Dr. McFarland personally and by untold numbers of those who admired him through his writings and accomplishments. This is his last important writing and as time lends perspective to his greatness in his many fields of endeavor, his book will retain the simple spirit of a man who loved flowers and loved the folks who enjoyed them with him.

R. C. ALLEN, *Executive Secretary*
American Rose Society.

Harrisburg, Pennsylvania
December 15, 1948

CONTENTS

CONTENTS

LIST OF ILLUSTRATIONS

MEMOIRS of a ROSE MAN
by J. Horace McFarland

My FATHER, a born teacher who also loved the land because he was born on a farm, carried his enthusiasms into the Civil War. He was the lieutenant colonel and most of the time the acting commander of a Pennsylvania regiment, and his meticulously written letters tell about occurrences in Virginia before the march to Gettysburg in June 1863 that ended his walking days. He wrote of the estates of the old F. F. V.'s for which he had to supply guards, and not the least interesting of his observations were those in which he envied the wealthy Virginians the food they ate while he and his officers' mess went almost hungry. There was no easy food supply in those wartime days.

He went to war in 1862 from a country academy in Pennsylvania, and when he came back on crutches he still loved the land. He told the five-year-old boy that I then was, how much he loved it and what it would do. In fact, as a result of this discussion I planted some seeds—I think corn—in a spot that I controlled, following exactly the instructions given. I watered the planting thoroughly and returning to the spot the next day, I seem to have done some weeping when I discovered that the seeds had not yet sprouted!

This I think was the beginning of my gardening. It was continued with further instructions and better results when we came to Harrisburg to live. Somewhere around 1868 my father's longing for the land pulled him out of the brick-row house we lived in, out to a partially abandoned place of several acres along the river front. Apples, pears, plums, quinces, and all the other tree fruits were growing there, including some elusive peaches, one of which, being grown from a seed, came to be known later as the "McFarland" peach.

In those days the Concord grape vied with the Isabella and the Clinton for home use, but the man who had planted the place had learned of what were known as the "Rogers hybrids," so he planted a vineyard, labeled only by the numbers attached to these hy-

Grapes have always found a loving and sustaining arbor in the garden at Breeze Hill. This is the CHARLES DOWNING variety

brids. I knew, for example, how large was the black "Rogers 19" and how sweet was amber "Rogers 3."

My father's energy was not satisfied with the publishing of a reform newspaper, so, loving the land as he did, he started the "Riverside Nurseries." I grew up in those nurseries,

4

which came to have several field branches contiguous to Harrisburg.

Now I was undergoing my four-year school experience during the development of the nurseries, and chemistry was the dream of my life. I hated the incidental work I had to do in and about the nursery and the green-houses, because the bottles, the liquids and the salts called me. Naturally I had to get acquainted with the land, and I grew seed-lings, budded peach trees and did the other things that came my way. Particularly I de-veloped the marketing of the Concord grapes in a vineyard branch which we had estab-lished, and had great pleasure in taking out daily a wagon load of fresh dewy grapes which still retained their bloom. Incidentally, there was one other vineyard which grew remark-able grapes, and it was owned by the man who built the house in which I now live at Breeze Hill.

So my horticultural beginnings were in the ground, though they switched over to the use of type, paper, ink and presses when my fa-ther's newspaper enterprise got me into the handling of type. The printing ink which stuck to my fingers still stays with me. It began because it seemed to me that I could make a better arrangement of certain catalogues I knew of if I set the type with my own hands, and so I did in these old days of wood cuts long before any color presses were evolved in America. My graduation through the garden and the nursery into the print-shop was merely a progression without much of a separation. It still operates that way, because now I make books and catalogues about and for gardens, and try them out to a very considerable extent at Breeze Hill. A side course in photography began when a New York publisher paid me for the first contribution I ever wrote, with a No. 1 Kodak, making on film a round picture 2½ inches in diameter. The camera got larger and heavier and the demands on it became greater. I well remember one early August day when I landed in Atlanta, Georgia, commissioned to photograph a great peach harvest. I had the usual suitcase, of course, but also a camera case, and I can still see the reproachful look I got from the darkey on the platform that hot, hot day when I responded to his "Take yo' grip,

Boss?" by handing him this camera case weighing 55 pounds!

I did see two thousand acres of peaches harvested, having previously seen the trees planted, as on various occasions I visited my friend Hale at Fort Valley, Georgia. That was a most hospitable place, and the fried chicken abundantly served seemed to find a proper place in my spare anatomy, because one time the cook ventured the inquiry "Is you got hollow legs, Boss?" when I came for the third supply.

By this time I was touching the land with my fingers and putting things into it. To be sure, I lived in a brick house, and with nothing but a back yard planted pretty nearly to its limit. The 55-pound camera case got toted pretty well over the United States while I was accumulating things that seemed to be needed for the catalogue and book business.

Lured by rumors of a great new process for color printing, and equally excited by possible contacts with that man who is the senior horticulturist of the United States today, Liberty Hyde Bailey, I went to New York and put a year into color study and advanced pho-

tography, together with other experiences
that may not here be mentioned. This
brought me back to Harrisburg with friend-
ships that still last. I came to know the really
great men who made the publishing frater-
nity of New York in those days. I knew the
printers, the color men, the artists, and I can
still recall with humble gratitude the kindness of a very great artist, F. Hopkinson
Smith, who taught me what color is and
how to use it.

Using the author's privilege, and showing
some respect for the equities of the situation,
I can say that our Harrisburg printshop kept
on doing catalogues and books. It produced
all the great cyclopedias which Bailey of Cornell added to orderly botanical literature. It
did many great books, and I think put a new
note into the catalogue part of horticulture
merchandising through its combination of
color and the new half tone of those days, to
take the place of the old woodcut.

All this brings me to the time when I could
return to that old Haehnlen place which has
been mentioned earlier as being a sort of
grape Heaven.

I CAME to Breeze Hill in 1909. My good wife, conscious of the fact that the house was on a hill (even though on the edge of a city with all the street names and "trimmings"), and remembering that a friend in central New York had a "Breeze Hill" estate, agreed that the name was appropriate. She also remarked that we would need to change only one letter in case we were frozen out that first winter! We never did freeze out. The name has come to mean something in consequence of my endeavors to have as many growing things as I could pack into 2.4 acres of city land. This was really the beginning of the suburban development called Bellevue Park, dependent for its design on the genius of the late Warren H. Manning.

So this story I have to tell must be quite personal, particularly in these days when I realize that a great many of my plant dreams have gone up in the genial glow of Breeze Hill's fireplace. Incidentally, with more than thirty years of this plant-packing endeavor, there has been much removal as well as much planting, so it has never been necessary to buy wood for open fires during about twenty of those years.

I was extremely fortunate in not having had a hard and fast fixed plan to work to. Mr. Manning did show me the vertical axis I needed to use, because he simply prolonged the line from the center of the great old living room in which the previously mentioned fireplace came to exist. The horizontal axis came naturally, because there had to be some way to get to other parts of this quarter-circle property, now surrounded by three paved city streets, in which it has been possible to locate more than 1300 species in some 350 genera.

Roses were nothing to worry about at the beginning, because there weren't any of them save a few ragged old plants that were an incidental part of the scanty plant population. There was what seemed to be a natural spread of forsythias that had "gone wild" and there were four or five great lilacs. The tree situation depended upon a great sycamore standing near the home, and giving me at the be-

11

ginning a persistent trouble because its leaves were attacked each season by an anthracnose which dropped them to the ground. It was soon found that if I wanted to keep the old tree alive I had to stop this trouble, and that has involved a Davey spraying-job which has made the sycamore an expensive but none the less precious luxury.

There were seven dominant horse chestnuts about the house, two of which promptly came down because we had to get light into the house. The five remaining have had to have much tree surgery, and they are, I presume, a great credit to the place, though needing now further reduction to admit more sunlight to the home. There had been a pear orchard, but the trees were all dead save two. Two persimmon trees (fortunately male and female) kept company with the sycamore, and there was a husky linden, that is now approximately sixty years old, which has proved to be a desirable tree. A group of sour cherries suggested that we could have pies, though to get in other things than cherries they have now been mostly removed. It was upon this foundation that, engaged as I am in the actual

Horse Chestnut Trees occupy a prominent place around the
house at Breeze Hill

business of printing horticultural books and catalogues, I began to build pictures to and from the house, and these have continued to be made, so that more than 50,000 photographs have resulted.

When the rose began to be exciting, Breeze Hill became a rose center, and roses flowed to it from all the world. Certain lovely Australian climbers and polyanthas are just as good this year as they seemed to be soon after their 1927 planting. Many hopeful rose growers with whom I came in contact after I began to make an Annual every year for the American Rose Society have sent me their productions, so that always from 50 to 100 numbered but unnamed roses are on trial, upon which I can do my share of criticizing toward the ideal rose conditions for America. I well remember when Los Angeles was merely Fred Howard's "No. 105."

We who lived in the old mansion house intended to eat from the garden as much as we could manage, and a good bit of fun followed the attempts to do things according to the prescriptions some of my college friends laid down. I remember my introduction to the unpleasant fungous disease "early blight," just when my attempt to grow potatoes up to the Cornell standards seemed most encouragingly successful. Like a thief in the night the fungus descended, and the pitiful remainder left me determined not to do much real farming in this little area. I do not grow potatoes, but I have sweet corn invariably.

But the other garden satisfactions have been mine, and I hope will continue to be. I shall probably mention from time to time some disappointing things that occurred, and I must in all frankness begin by stating that I have made all the mistakes I know about, with probably others to come, so that while there may be in the pages that follow suggestions of value, they are to be taken as experimental experiences rather than directions. What I shall write will be quite frank. It will also probably be influenced somewhat by what my many horticultural friends tell me, and the thousands who have visited Breeze Hill have contributed experiences well worth while to me, because they have increased the fun of living there. The visitors' book is always open in the rose house

15

and contains many names, some quite distinguished.

Lest there may be some misunderstanding, let me say that Breeze Hill was established at the tail-end of an old vineyard which had not been very liberally maintained. The soil is a rather heavy clay shale, with all too little humus. I started with the ideal that I would try to have a foot of arable soil all over the place, and my pocketbook soon bore witness to the cost of manure and other forms of plant food that would bring about this situation. There had been a sort of an entrance through hedges of arborvitae, and the previous owner had evidently become hard-boiled enough to cut these off brutally after they had grown to 7 or 8 feet. Many of them died and others twisted around into curious shapes, the result being that with the fortunate variation of about fifteen feet in level between the highest and the lowest portions of Breeze Hill I have had all sorts of contour problems to play with. When someone comes in these days and sees the really lovely rock garden which my late co-worker, Stevens, constructed, he is likely to say: "How fortunate it is that you have such a fine

The rock garden was an excellent way to utilize the site of an old greenhouse. No one enjoyed and appreciated it more than Dr. McFarland himself

limestone outcrop," to which I can truthfully reply that there was not a bit of limestone on the place over four inches in length, and that all the variety and beauty he sees are the result of one man's endeavor to find comfortable places in which the rock plants he came to love might grow. (Anyone who looks at the entrance to that rock garden from the higher level will find a little tablet, quite imperishable in nature, which tells the story of how it came about and who did it. I am not telling about my own plans, which did not tend toward rock gardens.)

Another remark which the casual visitor will probably make will be about the almost level Center Garden area, which may be looked over from the pleasant little rose house constructed of old cedar posts. He does not know that this was the basement of an old greenhouse which my predecessor had established, and that any time we dig deeply enough we may unearth some bit of greenhouse remainder. It was great fun to level this off and eventually, because we did want waterlilies, to cut down one end of it in order to obtain space for a lily pool, so built that the

A pool flanked with Iris in the foreground, and a sun dial occupying the focal point in the background, constitute the axis of the Peony Garden at Breeze Hill

necessary surrounding walls could take up some of the rock relations we needed if we were to keep on with rock plants. The connecting of this lily pool with "Steve's" rock garden and the necessary provision of a workyard, so that the utilities of the place might be unobtrusively served, has been a part of the experiences that I think have kept me alive way beyond the legitimate "three-score and ten" allotted to even a garden man.

When I began to think about Breeze Hill as an entity, and the advance of Bellevue Park settled the names of the three streets that bounded it, I first thought of a rose hedge that should encircle it all. Persuaded out of this, I did put in a barberry hedge, using the Thunberg barberry on the two long right angle lines and the common American barberry for the long curved line. These hedges prospered so much that when they began to take 4 to 8 feet inside the legitimate lines and I came to feel the need for more planting space, I had to take them out, which was quite a job of digging, dragging, cutting and contriving. Then I followed with the Japanese yew, or *Taxus cuspidata,* on two of the three boundary lines, and joined these two ends with a curved hedge which we call the "Walsh Memorial Hedge" of roses, concerning which the story may later be told in these pages.

But now we have the place enclosed, and what I may come to tell about it is with the lines thus established. I shall tell of various experiences and attempts, which still continue because I have no interest in a static garden. I ought to say, because of the publication relation which is entered into as these things go into print, that at least twenty years ago I stopped burning leaves and woody trash because I realized that I was destroying potential fertility. Enough space was taken for a great muck-pile on which all leaves and waste were and are deposited, to be wet and turned and made into the lovely leaf-mould that makes gardening easier and better.

---

*A*T ITS BEGINNING Breeze Hill had no climbing roses; now it has nearly 300 varieties growing under name and loving care, and numberless candidates ready to take the place of some one of the old group that isn't good enough to stay. These climbing roses mark the place from afar off, because they are trained carefully, though not expensively, on a system that developed itself under need. I found that I could buy gas pipe, or whatever the junkman had of the nature, in casual lengths that would make it possible for me to get the 8-foot standard I wanted, with no complication save cutting the pipe. A year or two of trial convinced me that rust could so weaken a pipe larger than one inch that it would break off, wherefore a plan was worked out so that each pipe is cast into a 4-inch concrete base of about 2 feet (the concrete being home-mixed and home-poured). There has

The SUNDAY BEST Rose was permitted to grow naturalistically in the garden at Breeze Hill. In its long graceful sweeps, it assigns all neighboring plants to a secondary place

been no failure among these posts in the last twenty-five years, and, under the system also added of adopting a certain height on the post when I might thread in a label arrangement, the question of the name of the variety has been rather permanently settled.

At first we planted the roses and let them grow a while before we put in the post; then we discovered that the post and the variety had better get along together, and so they do. With a natural preference for graceful curves, it was found that if we spaced these posts apart quite accurately and prepared the open ends as needed, we might spring a graceful and inexpensive strap-iron arch between two posts as a basis upon which to train the roses as they came along. Anyone visiting the Breeze Hill Garden will note that these arch supports for the climbing roses are pleasantly conspicuous, particularly in the late summer after the pruning has been done and the new shoots have started toward the next year's bloom.

There are of course many other ways to do this, some of them more expensive, but I have not seen any that gave a pleasanter effect or a better opportunity to make the rose prosper and do its very best.

As available space for more climbers gave out, the six foot separations were cut in half, and in some parts of the rose garden the graceful arches intersect quite agreeably and the roses do just as well at three feet as at six.

Because of the uses to which the garden is put for observation, photographing and record, it was suggested that we place the climbing roses according to pattern; that is, that we segregate all the pinks, all the yellows, and all the reds. That has been done, in the show garden at least, and again the effect is wholly pleasing to the eye and quite comfortable to the mind because the opportunity for comparison between roses of the same general color is convenient and constant.

Developing in the main garden, which we sometimes call the "West Garden," the larger plantings of hybrid tea, polyantha, and tea roses, we maintained a certain amount of agreeable relation between the climbing and the bush roses, again with good effect. Under the system which has just been suggested, space is saved, for while the climbing roses are

25

a full 6 feet, and indeed exactly 6 feet apart, the separations are ample and the ground below is left for the bush roses to be comfortably available to those who would see and compare.

One little bother has made some inconvenience. Not all roses called climbing roses are of the so-called rambler type with ability to make shoots 10 feet and more long. Some are truly pillar roses, and these expend their energies on the posts, with little disposition to climb the curved arches referred to. Theoretically this is quite a difficulty; practically it doesn't amount to anything, and it does afford occasion for some surprising things to happen, when what is expected to be a pillar rose with a height limit of 8 or 10 feet begins to reach out and possess the neighborhood! The long shoots can go either way at the top, and that leads to some interesting juxtapositions. This then is one of the reasons why this method of treating climbing roses is simple but productive of educational and pleasing results.

As will appear as we go along, roses are not starved at Breeze Hill—in fact, we have been

The beauty of Climbing Roses was everywhere apparent in the
Rose Garden at Breeze Hill. Simple, home-made supports made
it possible to display a great number of climbers

reproached by an eminent rose authority because he thinks we have given too much fertility to the soil and that we ought to restrict that fertility. So far as this concerns the climbers I won't pay any attention to it. Every climber has been set in a genuine pit dug out at least two feet down into the underlying shale, with drainage there provided if needed, and with good honest growing soil, fertilization and permanent sustentation taken into account. It is undoubtedly possible to fertilize the climbing roses after they have grown, but it has seldom seemed to be necessary because the original provision has been generous and the result satisfactory to all concerned.

Later on we will discuss the pruning of roses, but the general rule for the climbing roses that are the subject of this particular dissertation is to prune only once, and that is soon after the crop is over, or as near that time as we can get to it. This is done by removing any old and worn-out shoots and carefully tying into place the young growth that shows a desire to go on. Under this method there is constant and adequate renewal, and I could take a visitor to many roses that have been in one spot for twenty years and are full of growing, vigorous life right now.

I have had to absorb with some little difficulty the idea that given a good plant, fertile soil, decent treatment, the rose wants to stay, and that the hard-boiled prescriptions made by some rose people are more interesting than they are important. Any real rose lover will soon find that the community of interest which arises under the circumstances mentioned above, means that he can get good roses and enjoy them without too much scientific diversion, and with almost no attention to rigid restrictions.

N what I am about to write concerning the use of climbers in the garden, I shall be making very little reference to those than can readily be obtained from seed annually. I love a morning glory, but I do not think any who will read these words need to be introduced to its easy supply, or indeed, under some conditions, to the danger that it will become almost indigenous by self-seeding and have to be rooted out later. There are a number of excellent vines that can be grown from seed, and the better seed catalogues are quite full of suggestions which will count favorably toward getting a good show. It is hard to stay off sweet peas in this connection, because I have succeeded and failed so many times with them, and am now growing the new All-America Trials because I feel committed to that superb attempt by seedsmen and gardeners to get the best. I could cover the subject of sweet peas by saying that they are a grand good thing to have if you can make them behave for you. And I congratulate in advance anyone who has no bother with mosaic or those other troubles which disastrously interfere with sweet pea pleasure.

But it is rather the hardy vines I would discuss, and I will begin with one of the hardiest (some would say the worst) of them — the honeysuckles. I have read much about creating a nuisance by planting honeysuckles, and I have also lived with the family, as evidenced in the easiest and best variety, *Lonicera japonica* (also called *L. Halliana*). This came to us, I presume, from Japan, as I find it credited to eastern Asia. It has many subvarieties, and most gardens have had the one that used to be freely sold as *L. Halliana*. This honeysuckle is almost evergreen, but even if it does not hold its leaves over winter, they come again very promptly in the spring. In various forms it is a facile and to me pleasing ground cover which can be depended upon, once it is started, to cover all the ground it can reach, while at the same time it yields to that sort of sane weeding which is the essence of getting along with plants. I think it was in Delaware that I traveled

31

through a region where this Japanese honeysuckle had been permitted to run at random—and it had gone far and fast. There it
was both a pest and a witness to thoughtless
gardening.

There are at least a hundred species of
this *Lonicera* genus, many of which grow
prostrate, while others make great and admirable bushes. The sane use of the creep-
ing honeysuckles is as cover plants, planned
to do a definite thing and kept as much in
place as is grass or any other ground cover.
I did have at one time *L. Halliana pileata,*
which had pleasing yellow flowers, but that
one concluded not to stay with me. I now
enjoy certain of the taller species which make
easily trained bushes up to six feet and more
in height. In full growing time these will
have plenty of very fragrant and very pleasing
flowers in shades not provided by any other
easily grown vine. Honeysuckles can be a
very admirable garden facility, and can also,
as I have written, be a nuisance in the hands
of careless gardeners. Anyone who reads these
words and wants to make a trial can usually
get a start from some friend, or from a nurs-

Honeysuckle (*Lonicera*) gracing one of the entrances to Dr. McFarland's home. The hardy climbers found a generous welcome in Breeze Hill

ery which will give him his own choice as between the climbing and standing varieties. After that it is up to him.

If I took only my own experiences and preference into account, I would have to say that the clematis is the aristocrat of the climbing vines available to us in the northern United States. To be sure, a louder color noise is made, where it is hardy, by bougainvillea, of which, in addition to the blatant magenta-hued flower bracts that one finds everywhere in the South, there are much finer sorts, one of which is known as Crimson Lake bougainvillea. This is literally superb in every respect. I count as one of my own cherished possessions a vine of it that reminds us of summer as it grows all winter in a little greenhouse heated just enough to keep my automobile from freezing.

But the clematis family need yield to nothing. *Clematis paniculata,* which came to us from Japan, provides a grand early fall coverage of well-shaped white blossoms. These are profusely displayed on a vine that completely covers any available surface. One could not miss looking at it, because his nose

Dr. McFarland considered Clematis the aristocrat of northern
U. S. hardy climbers. *Clematis Jackmani* is perhaps the finest
of all the large-flowered varieties

is aware of it long before he sees it. There is a peculiarly rich and pleasing fragrance belonging to this clematis.

There are other sorts of this white-flowering type, but not one of them compares with *C. paniculata* in real beauty value, and particularly fragrance. I do not go on with the varieties, because I cannot see the use of suggesting other than the best.

Other very refined and somewhat difficult varieties derive mostly from England. Most garden travelers have chanced upon a great display of *C. jackmani,* which might stand as the head of all these foreign-born items, showing flowers three inches or more across, of a deep and brilliant purple. This and its friends are in what is called the large-flowered class, and those wonderfully successful growers in Central New York, the Georges of Fairport, have caused them to flourish to the delight of other garden lovers. They run to brilliant colors, and while not altogether easy to grow, are worth more than twice the trouble ever put upon them. Anyone who has been able to get a plant of *Prins Hendrik* or *Nellie Moser* started will be much more

than satisfied when it blooms, and it blooms
long. As I am not writing a catalogue I cannot name all the others that I have known
and loved—and sometimes lost—but I do
know that such sorts as *Mme. Edouard André,
King Edward VII* and related species are a
guerdon of success to any gardener.

Then there are the easy varieties, both
American and foreign, which are used in the
propagation of the finer sorts I have before
mentioned. To anyone who is enticed into
clematis culture by what I write let me suggest that he get a few selected healthy plants
that will begin for him the procession that
he will never relinquish cheerfully. It is of
no particular importance to your garden or
mine that the lovely flowers I see are grown
on grafted plants; the essential thing for me
to do is to get them and care for them. There
are American sorts that are quite easy to
have. I have seen them grow wild in Texas.
I grew up knowing these lovely little tubular
flowers as *C. coccinea,* but I am now corrected
to know that I must call them *C. texensis.*
Quite as pleasing is another native which
happens to have purplish recurved flowers

and much fragrance. It is *C. crispa.* Neither of these fine American plants is hard to have, and I think both of them have given rise to hybrids which will tempt the clematis lover once he gets started.

I have found that the clematis enjoys half shade, such as I find at Breeze Hill in the shadow of certain tall arborvitae, but I have taken care that there is depth of soil that belongs to the clematis rather than to the arborvitae, and a little lime in the soil. With some study and investigation one can get started in three groups and discover whether he is to have a definite woody climbing friend, or one pleasantly shrubby and herbaceous. My whole thought in these words is to get some people to enjoying a very delightful climbing vine and its herbaceous friends.

Because I have been writing about climbers, I have not taken into account the shrubby forms of clematis, admirable in themselves and worth cultivating as one gets acquainted with this extremely rich and varied species of wide reach. Nor have I tried to bring in certain Chinese immigrants that really show attractive yellow flowers on a

Wisteria making a rampant growth over an arbor in the garden
at Breeze Hill. This view stresses the simplicity which prevailed
in Dr. McFarland's garden

decent vine. Anyone who likes the family and begins to work with it will not require further inducement to go on with it. My hope has been to suggest a few of the less familiar items that are good to grow in the hands of those who love fine things, after which the plant adventure that is really the basis of garden advance goes on.

I have not said a thing about what is our most familiar vine, the wisteria. It is possibly wise for me to admit at the outset that this is a strong but freaky vine. It can grow furiously and fast and provide, if it is suited, very beautiful and tremendously long terminal racemes such as for many years have astonished those who have visited Japan. Yet our common and easy American form, which is really the Chinese wisteria, can afford immense satisfaction either in its white or purple forms. There are those who tell me I should use a sharp spade to cut the roots of the wisterias that do not bloom. I do not like to do this.

There is a trumpet vine that provides splendid foliage and great clusters of orange-scarlet flowers. In its *Mme. Galen* variety it does bloom differently to great advantage. This bignonia, sometimes called tecoma, is a grand thing for an old tree stump or a rock pile, which it will cover with summer glory.

One cannot keep away from the so-called Virginia creeper family that the botanists have called *Parthenocissus* but the tradesmen have grown and sold as *Ampelopsis*. The one we know easiest has its leaf described with the specific name of *quinquefolia*. This is an old reliable that can be counted upon to stay with the garden and do much toward its beauty. It has a form called Lowi that has leaves only an inch and a half long. The twigs of this splendid vine adhere to any substance they cover, and the vine can be used as a tracery on walls or for any other purpose that suggests garden refinement.

The Silver Lace Vine, *Polygonum auberti,* is refined as to flower, but rather coarse in its growth. It makes a superb covering vine, particularly if a location is chosen with more shade than sun. It belongs to a rather pervading family and on any sign of dominance, may need to be rooted out completely.

I have seen some fine examples of the

Dutchman's Pipe, a rather unpleasant name for *Aristolochia sipho*. This is a vigorous plant with very large leaves, uniform in character and affording a unique decorative effect. It is worthwhile for a bold spot.

To omit the evergreen climbing vines would be unfortunate. Most people know what is called hardy ivy—*Hedera helix* by botanical designation — but not everyone knows that there are many varieties, some not so hardy. This vine clings in a most interestingly peculiar fashion to the surface it is to cover, and some of the sorts are of particular elegance in appearance. I have found it not only good as a low-climber, but particularly valuable to cover a slope where no grass could be grown because conditions were too shady. The ivy makes its own shade, to be sure, but it also gives a notable elegance of covering where it does its splendid work. At Breeze Hill vines planted without much care on a slope that was almost grassless have now provided an admirable bank of hardy ivy. It is pleasant to walk upon; it can actually be mowed if that is desirable. I like this use of it and so do garden visitors.

There is a wild vine, if one might properly so call it, that tends in the fall to throw garlands of scarlet and orange fruits overhead along the woodland ways. This is *Celastrus scandens,* the familiar bittersweet. If one is fortunate enough to get a seedling of creditable parentage and a tendency toward making large seeds, it is a very well worthwhile vine. If, on the contrary, the fruits are diminutive, the vine is best thrown away.

Those who become a little climber-wise will want more of the same, and that can be accomplished by reading the carefully made catalogues that are now available. The experiment is worth while and successes are frequent.

$\mathcal{O}$NE of the most fruitful and active amateur rose growers I have ever known was Dr. Edmund M. Mills, who was also quite a successful Methodist pastor. His organizing ability had caused him to be selected as the secretary of the General Conference of the Methodist Episcopal Church for twenty years (before it got rid of the "Episcopal" in its title.) I knew him as a district superintendent most of this time in the neighborhood of Syracuse, New York. He was making roses live the gospel around the churches and his influence is yet felt, for I do not think he ever preached a sermon or made a visitation which did not in some way include a reference to the queen of flowers. As a matter of fact, a Van Fleet rose was named for him, but it has never been sufficiently popular to properly support this great man's fame. His Methodist

rose persuasions resulted in the planting of a very beautiful public rose garden in Thornden Park, Syracuse, and one of my golden memories is attendance upon the dedication of that garden.

This preacher-rose man was an inimitable raconteur, as was proved to me one memorable day when several rose addicts gathered at the invitation of a fourth (an even more serious addict) to see the great roses he was growing in Richmond, Indiana. Every day a great flood of roses was shipped from there to attempt to sweeten the air of Chicago. At Richmond "Gurney" Hill, as he liked to be called, and his son "Joe" were the rose growers and the hosts on this famous day.

Gurney Hill was an extensive and very successful rose hybridizer, his aim being to grow not only beautiful flowers but strong and vigorous plants that would prosper under the ideal greenhouse conditions he provided for them. Thus their beneficence could be extended over the whole winter. Some of the most effective and prominent roses of the present day such as "Better Times" had their beginnings in the many acres of glass-covered

45

Dr. Edmund M. Mills, rose-growing preacher, who was a pioneer
in the breeding of roses

garden that Mr. Hill had brought into beautiful bloom.

It was at this astonishing place that I got an idea of what it means and costs to try for better roses. After no end of crossing and hybridizing, Mr. Hill obtained one year about 15,000 seedlings, which he promptly selected down to less than 200 to go on with. He felt he was really "going places" with roses when he got out of this expensive effort one rose particularly adapted to his sedulously maintained ideals. When one wandered through his great greenhouses, where it was possible actually to get under overhanging rose branches full of lovely bloom, one appreciated the devotion involved in this broad advance. To be sure, he was aiming for greenhouse standards, but I have yet to find a good greenhouse rose that is not also a good garden rose.

He brought from England the rose Ophelia, which was the beginning of a great race of greenhouse and garden roses. In fact, when he first found this rose in the hands of William Paul, its originator in England, he tried his best to get possession of all of the

Dr. Edmund M. Mills Rose, a hybrid between *Rosa hugonis* and *R. altaica,* is a vigorous shrub rose of great beauty

plants, so that he could have the exclusive market in America. On the memorable occasion to which I have referred we were participating in the advance of the Ophelia strain, which, by the way, is recorded in *Modern Roses III* as the parent of 28 sports and hybridized seedlings.

Most of us like to eat turkey, and in these post-war days, with hoofed meat beyond our pocketbooks, we are glad for such dinners. It was an interesting day when I visited these Hill greenhouses at Richmond, Indiana, particularly as I was with Dr. Mills, the rose-growing preacher, and the subject of this sketch. The gathering of rose men occurred at the appointed time when Dr. Mills, Samuel S. Pennock, the Quaker treasurer of the American Rose Society, Robert Pyle, a world-traveling rose merchant, and I were the guests of the two Hills in Richmond. We visited all morning in rosy discussion, and were not surprised when Mrs. "Joe" Hill invited us to dinner—at noon, if you please. She did not disclose to us the fact that it was going to be turkey. We ate joyously, the big delicious dinner being illuminated by much rose conversation and the expert story-telling of Dr. Mills. Then came more greenhouses and more roses. "Mother" Hill insisted on having us to dinner that evening just before we were to take the night train for Chicago. Behold, it was another turkey feast, and the good lady was not behind her son's wife in a disposition to "feed the animals." I did the best I knew with the situation, but I surely had enough turkey! All the time we ate, a steady stream of amusing stories came from the preacher. Replete with turkey, we took the train for Chicago.

Arriving there early on Sunday morning, there was consultation in the station. I had made in advance an arrangement to go out to Egandale to see a great gardener who had defied successfully the winds of Lake Michigan. Dr. Mills had planned to attend a Methodist service in the Auditorium. When he heard me make by telephone an arrangement with Mr. Egan to be met at Highland Park, he decided that he preferred the garden to the church.

As we were met at the train by Mr. Egan,

Dr. Mills said to me plaintively: "Now, Dr. McFarland, don't you get me started at Egan's place; I'm tired, and you know I oughtn't to talk all day." But I had to tell him that he had always been an effective self-starter. Certainly I didn't have to do any "starting" because Dr. Mills himself was reminded of something before we left the Highland Park station, and he kept on being reminded of things all that memorable day. Story after story came from him, even the story of a wedding in one of his pastorates that took twenty-four hours to complete . . . . .

We survived the stories, the lovely gardens and the courteous hospitality, all of which joined in making up an enduring memory of two unique days in the lives of four real rose men. (But we did have too much turkey.)

WHAT has the Department of Agriculture had to do with roses? So far as actual publication is concerned, the honest answer would have to be "Nearly nothing." To be sure, the Federal Department of Agriculture has done vast good in publishing for Americans the details of new plant discoveries all over the world. For many years it made an annual offer of plants and seeds from various locations, as reported by its agents. No names were attached to the items thus covered, and when you selected the numbers that looked interesting, you might eventually share in the extremely limited propagation conducted by the Department at Glenn Dale, a farm located between Baltimore and Washington. Here came the treasures of the Orient, and indeed of the Occident, and to a plant-hungry mind a visit to Glenn Dale was an event to remember.

Now the propagation at Glenn Dale was conducted under the eye of a great master of horticulture who had hidden himself there. He was Dr. Walter Van Fleet, a New Yorker by birth. This man was a born scientist. He knew birds and butterflies, and came to know related plants as well. With other good men he gravitated into the Bureau of Plant Industry in Washington, and then became associated with the Federal trial plots at Glenn Dale. Desiring to be completely independent, he bought for his own home a tract of land adjoining the government land, and there built the house where I so gladly visited. Thus this true scientist, who was only incidentally a medico, made himself independent of the Federal Government, while very thoroughly serving it in the origination and introduction of new plants. He was interested in the rose, and he was just as much interested in the betterment of many other items of the flower garden—cannas, gladiolas, dahlias—as he was in strawberries, gooseberries, corn, tomatoes, etc. I came to know that he had a definite rose ideal to work toward, which was roses that would bloom all the growing season, and so take care of themselves that there might be beauty every growing day. (If he were alive now I know he would be working with two or three other scientists for the eradication of the dreaded black-spot through microscopic investigation and the development of resistant strains.)

Dr. Van Fleet had a season of association at the curious community of Ruskin, Tenn., where came such men as the Russian prince Kropotkin and the then famous journalist Arthur Brisbane. He also had to do there with David Fairchild, who in these days is maintaining at the very southern tip of Florida an astonishing garden that is bringing rare treasures of the tropics to America. It was in a letter from Dr. Fairchild that information came concerning two roses that really started at Ruskin and have since fortuitously possessed all America in the direction of Dr. Van Fleet's aims. In the early days of this century, a rose bloomed that seemed to this scientist close to his ideal. He and his good wife agreed, when it bloomed, to call it Daybreak. It pleased those who saw it. At about that time contact was made with the Henderson firm in New York and they bought all the plants save one, which the

Doctor held for his own pleasure. Endeavoring to speed up propagation, the New York firm lost all its plants, and later obtained a renewed stock arising from the one plant Dr. Van Fleet had retained. It seemed appropriate to the Henderson people to call the rose Dr. W. Van Fleet, and so it has remained.

Just about this same time there came through the hybridizers' hands an astonishing white rose, nearly single, to which the name Silver Moon was attached. Meantime international disturbances caused the Doctor to do some hybridizing with Japanese sources. The result was a rose that, when I saw a great plant of it at West Grove, Pennsylvania, was appropriately bearing the name American Pillar. Good as it is, Dr. Van Fleet, if he had lived, would certainly have carried it along, pursuing his ideals not only of strength, resistance and other good qualities, but of constant blooming.

In those days some of us believed we could have the iron curtain removed that restrained world introductions of the Department of Agriculture, since these resulted from the scientific efforts of great practitioners. I well

Mary Wallace was one of the first of Dr. Van Fleet's ideals as "dooryard" roses to come into production

remember the situation when once I went to Glenn Dale in Dr. Van Fleet's absence to see a gorgeous rose blooming at its beautiful best, row upon row. I took an armful of these roses with me to Washington, where another great distributing rose man, S. S. Pennock, took care of them over night. The next day, with Robert Pyle, I took that rose to the office of the Secretary of Agriculture, Henry Wallace, father of Henry Agard Wallace. I told him of its origin and informed him that a few plants had been distributed for testing purposes. The result was that when exhibited in Portland, Oregon, it was daringly named for Wallace's daughter.

Thus the Mary Wallace is one of the first of Dr. Van Fleet's ideals as "dooryard" roses to come into production. The Secretary also agreed that a contract might be made with the American Rose Society for the distribution of this rose, so that a good thing need not be officially lost. It so happened through an extremely liberal contract with a grower in Texas (who carried propagating wood home in a suitcase) that it was possible to sell at a uniform price, and on agreed-upon terms,

57

Sᴀʀᴀʜ Vᴀɴ Fʟᴇᴇᴛ is a true tribute to the wife of the great rose breeder

propagating stock that really gave this rose its start.

Fortunately at about this time a letter was written by a Department of Agriculture authority permitting this beneficent arrangement to continue, so several other excellent roses were distributed. All of the results were used by the American Rose Society to advance the love of roses in America through the study of disease-control methods. There came along in due course Heart of Gold, a single rose that did not make good on its parentage, and a Rugosa hybrid, Sarah Van Fleet, that was a true tribute to the splendid woman who stood with Dr. Van Fleet during all this effort.

Then followed the Dr. E. M. Mills, named for the astonishing preacher who combined his Methodist preaching and practicing with his love of roses. This rose, joining the blood of a rose of Chinese parentage, *Rosa Hugonis*, with that of a Scotch native, *R. altaica*, did not make the grade, nor did the next number of this participating group, Breeze Hill, which had bestowed upon it the name of my garden home. This was the first one of a

series intended to bring into the potent Wichuraiana strain the rich colors of the French
roses. It did moderately well until shoulder-
ed out by the flood of new things that could
be more profitably grown.

Another one of these hardy climbing roses
in the "dooryard" class was raised by Dr. Van
Fleet in a hybrid between the Japanese Wichuraiana and a French Tea rose, Isabella
Sprunt. It produces one fine crop of sunny
tinted blooms, but they soon pass to white,
and it has not held out against competition.
However, my own bush at Breeze Hill is
highly prized.

Politics and roses do not hybridize with
great success and in recent years the Department of Agriculture has not gone on with
hybridization, principally because there is
not now in the work such a genius as was Dr.
Van Fleet. Its station at Glenn Dale is no
longer the dominant one; at a very great
establishment in Beltsville, Maryland, fine
things are done, and there may yet be wonderful results resting actually on the base established by men like Fairchild and Van Fleet.
At one of the annual meetings of the Ameri-

can Rose Society in Washington one of these Beltsville investigators, Thomas M. Little, Assistant Geneticist in the Bureau of Plant Industry, gave a complete presentation on "The Distribution of North American Rose Species." He showed by means of a series of maps that roses are found in every section from the Arctic Circle to Mexico, and that not one state in the United States nor one province in Canada is without its wild roses.

Another interesting presentation at this same annual meeting was that made by Dr. Charles E. Resser of the United States National Museum, to show that the rose was a dominating part of the growing world's economy thirty-five million years ago, and that, quoting Dr. Resser, "When man arrived on the earth, there was the beauty and fragrance of the rose to make his home most enjoyable."

*A*MONG the great greenhouse flower growers the name of E. Gurney Hill of Richmond, Indiana, will always be written with a smile. He had that smile, and all who had to do with him felt better because he beamed that smile at fellow flower-lovers.

But I was thinking when I started this sketch about a real master of horticulture whose name is perpetuated in the great Henderson firm of New York. He loved flowers and plants and trees and bulbs, and he wrote readily about them. More than that, he loved to talk with those who were eager to tap his stores of knowledge and he was always kindly.

When as a young printer I went to the first meeting of the Society of American Florists in Chicago one year, I was present in body but about a thousand miles away from having any real touch with the people there. One day as I sat wishfully thinking in the long hallway that then was the entrance to the

Palmer House, a tall Scotchman stopped and spoke to me. I did not need to be introduced to Peter Henderson, for it happened that my father had returned from England in his company one time many years before, and he knew what my name meant. He spent not more than ten minutes with me, but he so took my personality apart and shook it together that when I left him I was ready to make contacts with the florists to learn what they had to sell and to find out if they wanted to sell it. He was a most encouraging and friendly gentleman, and I think he was truly a mind reader.

Another similar contact was made when, also as a young catalogue printer, I paid a visit to the home of the great firm—now extinct, alas—which carried on the Mount Hope Nurseries in Rochester, New York. I had been in the office, which had no printing for me to do, when the electric spark of personality passed from a kindly man who was in that office and touched me. He was Mr. George Ellwanger, one of the members of the firm, and something I said made him realize that I wanted plant introductions. He took me out into their superb grounds and introduced me to the considerable population of evergreens growing there in such perfection. He stimulated my mind until I had a question about plants every minute, and I left his genial presence with that feeling of high thankfulness that always follows the doing or the receiving of a good deed. There had been no pressure of business relationship, nor did I want any after having made the acquaintance of so many pines and spruces and retinosporas in the company of this man who had planted them.

What a Great Garden Woman Can Do

There are in existence certain books ascribed·to "Neltje Blanchan," which was the pen name of an extraordinary garden woman. She was also bird lover, observer, mother, friend and garden enthusiast. The daughter of an important Holland family, she came into contact with the budding young publisher, Frank N. Doubleday, and the usual thing happened, for I firmly believe that gardens do bring good people together. I think of her often and of the kindness with which she handled me one time when I was building-worn and business-worn. It happened in the course of a trip I made to Nassau, after a bad session with what was then a new disease, "grippe." At the time I was printing a magazine, *Country Life in America,* and really participating in its editorial progress. Mr. Doubleday, a genial, friendly man, lived not far from the New York office that issued the magazine, and this great good woman (who happened also to be good-looking) maintained "open house" every Wednesday afternoon for the magazine folk. She knew how to get the best out of each man, and it was in the old Fourteenth Street house that Rudyard Kipling went through a siege of illness, and it was Mrs. Doubleday who kept him alive.

On the occasion I mention the Doubledays, worn with winter, had gone by random ways to Nassau. They had two adopted sons, and these boys didn't like the great hotel into which they had been suddenly dropped. Being of an adventurous and vigorous habit of mind and body, they asked the first good-

The Doubleday family at Nassau. Mrs. Doubleday (center) was an extraordinary garden woman

looking man they met on the street where they could find a place to live outside the city of Nassau, somewhere on the island of New Providence. From this inquiry came the transfer of the family residence to what was then called Long Branch, which was really along an exquisitely beautiful portion of the bay front of the city of Nassau, under active British domination. It was from there that Mr. Doubleday cabled me "Come down here with us, and you'll live a thousand years!" When I arrived at their friendly, simple home I found this good lady ready to mother me into health. I managed to forget "la grippe" in record time, and with this Yankee family ate, slept, bathed and boated happily in that kindly and beautiful climate. For formality we included a visit to the opening session of the miniature British Parliament that was part of the governmental machinery. This indeed was the only sight I have ever had of our British friends, with complete independence, using high hats and red coats to such advantage.

I have mentioned Mrs. Doubleday because she was a real garden woman as well as much else that brought her close to birds and nature. She has long gone to her reward, as has her husband, but so long as I live her memory will be precious to me as one of those folk with whom the garden has put me in touch to make my stay on this planet one of pleasantness.

LSEWHERE in these somewhat ran-
dom sketches I have told the story of the Mary
Wallace rose. In the same series of hybridi-
zations by Dr. Van Fleet other roses followed,
and disappointments also followed.

For example, there came one rose, under
the label W. S. 5, that seemed to be a promis-
ing plant. When it first bloomed and received the name of Heart of Gold, it looked
as if we were getting a real hybrid between
Rosa wichuraiana, the pugnacious and useful
Japanese rose, and the rather wonderful big
scarlet *Rosa moyesi.* It did bloom just that
way, giving single, open crimson blooms,
shading to white at the center, with conspicuous yellow stamens. The plant was vigorous,
and it kept blooming for about three weeks,
but it could not pass the standard which some
thousands of American rose lovers had built
up, and it has dropped out. It was a disappointment.

If this rose had happened to be selected by

HEART OF GOLD is a hybrid between *Rosa wichuraiana* and *R. moyesi* which at first was considered an outstanding creation

Luther Burbank during his singular lifetime at Santa Rosa, California, it would have been boomed and boomed as a "new creation," particularly as its percentage was so clear and important. It happens that at the very beginning of the Burbank excitement, I as a rose man investigated the situation, and found that there was none of the thoughtful and truly scientific method of hybridization characteristic of Dr. Van Fleet ever attributed to any of Burbank's work. His idea was to plant a very large quantity of rose seeds originated pretty much at random, and then hope that there would be some good items, as occasionally there were. I soured on the situation when I got a catalogue from Mr. Burbank in which he had, on one page, four roses that were "the best ever." Not one of them has since proved really worthwhile. I dropped the relationship after a curious conference that occurred in Hartford, Connecticut, in which a real expert from the Department of Agriculture, Dr. Liberty Hyde Bailey, the great fruit grower J. H. Hale, and I joined to study certain new Burbank offerings. We could not find anything to justify the state-

ments he made about his productions. He
was probably the most completely self-
deceived plantsman we have ever had in
America.

Burbank was not the only disappointment
I have encountered in my forty years of gardening. Desiring not to say unpleasant things
of anyone, I shall not name those whose ambition overran their judgment and who introduced new things that were not good enough
to be introduced. It was to avoid disappointments that the American Rose Society originated, more than twenty years ago, the department called "The Proof of the Pudding,"
in which those who love new roses tell of
their experience with them. This department,—in the 1947 Annual it occupies 54
pages, within which 147 persons tell their
own stories of the roses they have grown—has
come to be a valuable check on disappointment. Not many of the 9,000 members of
this virile organization fail to refer to "The
Proof of the Pudding" concerning any rose
that is newly offered them. If the location
of the approving or disapproving commenta-
tors is taken into account, there can be used

a very high grade of good judgment to avoid disappointments.

Although it is not exactly appurtenant to the title of this chapter, I feel like mentioning the gratification I find at the absence of boom prices among roses. There are many good things for the garden, including iris, peonies, gladiolus and other subjects of easy propagation, where these individual varieties are offered at prices from one dollar to $50 or more. I remember only one rose offered at $5 and it did not sell. The sound, sane practice has prevailed that when a man who raises roses has one that he believes in, he proceeds to propagate a considerable quantity, which sometimes means as many as 100,000 of a kind, and these can then be offered at a reasonable price. This provides the money that the grower needs and does not induce disappointment.

It happens that the same general relationship has become current when those who raise new roses arrange with trusted friends all over the country to receive and grow these in sufficient supply to give them a fair and square trial in comparison with other roses.

This avoids disappointment and promotes the easy and proper circulation of a meritorious new variety. These trials are called the "All America" trials.

I admit that roses are patented, and this is not the place to discuss the patent relationship, but inasmuch as the patent merely gives a platform to stand on when dishonorable practices ensue, the Government itself doing absolutely nothing to support it, it may be seen that it is only a mild protection. Almost no difficulties have occurred since the patent privileges were first made available to rose growers. The merit of the process appears to be the fact that a man's mental property is protected while he is developing it. He can maintain his price for several years while making the variety known, with some advantage to him by reason of the protection afforded by the patent. If he asks too high a price for his rose, he just doesn't sell it.

HE NAMES of these rose worthies who have passed on come before me in this attempt to give personality to some of the roses that still grow. I think with warm regard of these men with whom I worked by mail, although I seldom saw them face to face:

A. J. FISH

FOR MANY successive years I managed to see the Boston Flower Show, conducted by the Massachusetts Horticultural Society, and I would have had to be very blind if I had not noted that A. J. Fish of New Bedford, Mass., was sure to walk away with one or more of the best awards made in Boston, because of the climbing roses he showed. It was in 1916 that he told how he did it and why "the growing of climbing roses for exhibition is a very pleasant habit. To be successful you must grow a little better flowers than the other fellow." Then he told of his methods and gave lists of the varieties he had used, as written by him for the 1920 American Rose Annual. A striking thing in his statement is that "Indeed, roses look better picked and well set up than they do on the bushes."

In a letter written for the 1922 American Rose Annual he admitted that he had been specializing in hardy climbing roses for twelve years, and he added a startling statement: "One rose I never will have in my garden, as it is a leper, a mildew breeder—the old Crimson Rambler." However, it is only proper to say that there is now a rose of the same color that is not a leper, the Variety Chevy Chase, originated by N. J. Hansen at Dr. Whitman Cross's home in Chevy Chase, Maryland.

In another article Mr. Fish touched me off to great fondness for one of the less well known and yet finest climbers, the Zephirine Drouhin. This is an unusual Boursault rose bearing large pink and very fragrant flowers, which I now cherish yearly at Breeze Hill not only for its color but for its general aristocracy of appearance when in bloom.

Mr. Fish kept right along after the new

roses of his time, and he had no hesitation in commenting fully on the habits of the roses and his own habits of growing them. In one of his articles he disposes of the matter of protection when he says, "All the protection I give my climbers is horse manure, applied after the ground is frozen, and one of my heresies is that horse manure is better than cow manure for roses." Then he goes on to tell of his start with Silver Moon and Dr. Van Fleet. He tells of growing M. H. Walsh's ramblers, about which I will comment later, and of disregarding them because they bloomed too late. What he writes most intimately makes real to me a feeling I am cautious about thus putting into print—that roses recognize the grower and do better for the man who loves them. Certainly Mr. Fish raised his roses that way.

W. C. EGAN

VERY MUCH in the public garden prints of his time was a man who lived not far from Chicago, and whom it seemed very much worth while to hunt up. I discovered that Mr. Egan had found Highland Park to be

The SILVER MOON ROSE, a favorite of A. J. Fish, the New England grower who knew that rambler roses thrive best with plenty of compost in the soil

just outside the curtain of sooty smoke that shrouded Chicago itself, and that Egandale was a most notable garden. It was good at any time of the year but particularly when its genial proprietor could turn his fine Irish smile on a visitor. I acquired the habit of going to see him whenever I could. Always I found that he had done something with a plant that added to my deficient knowledge and that was obviously giving pleasure to others. It was at Egandale that I saw a rose that I found had been named Max Graf. It was growing in a great heap on his lawn when I first came under its influence. On that day in late June it was a mass of splendid single pink flowers amid glossy green leaves that were in themselves highly decorative. This rose, I discovered, was not of Mr. Egan's origination. But it might have been credited to him as introducer because everyone who saw it wanted it. It had slipped out into commerce and plants were obtainable. I pursued its origin, and found that a man in Massachusetts whose name was Bowditch had combined either or both *Rosa rugosa* and *R. wichuraiana* with our splendid American native *R. setigera.* This rose was therefore an international flower. It interested me particularly because it was such a grand ground cover, and as I came to know it later, my interest grew. I discovered that I could grow it in about thirty per cent access to sunlight and so it now lives at Breeze Hill. In the books it is called a Hybrid Rugosa, but a better name is given as it is designated "a valuable hardy ground cover." So it is, and I have seen no similar rose quite so persistently beautiful and dependable.

One of the things that bothered me at Egandale was the way in which Mr. Egan managed to grow in his little postage-stamp greenhouse plants of certain weeping fuchsias that overflowed the pots in which they were started. Consequently coming to his home one would find four or five great masses of fuchsias on the front porch. He did things like that all the time with many plants because he was a plant lover. As I have heretofore indicated, I have a firm belief that plants recognize the man with the loving hand and the kindly eye.

W. C. Egan had many garden friends. I

81

do not think any man ever got away from his garden without something to remember it by, in addition to what he had seen with his eyes and stored away in his head. There was always a cutting or a pot or something to indicate the Egan influence.

ARE YOU A GARDEN PERSONALITY?

I CAN answer this query by saying that if the only basis of a gardener is to imitate the work of someone else, there is no danger that the personality impression will be made. If, however, the gardener, be it man or woman, finds some one thing that particularly attracts him, and develops study and experiment leading toward knowledge, the personality issue is almost certain to be affirmative.

In my own generation of gardening I have had contact with scores, if not hundreds, of such personalities. It has been a great delight not only to read what these friends write, but when they visit Breeze Hill or I visit their gardens, to exchange experiences. Almost the first thing I undertake when I am visited at Breeze Hill is an inquiry into what that particular visitor really cares for in the garden. Inasmuch as Breeze Hill is not just a mere rose garden but an excellent general garden, with a great many things that reflect my own interests in items that are new or good or different, I don't often miss it.

This, therefore, is a plea for the development of sound personality. Somewhere else I am sure I have written of the personality that obtained rather humorous if not ludicrous expression when a man was so much in love with Hydrangea Peegee that he planted the whole of his yard with that vigorous shrub. He had constructed a curious kind of desert, without any of the advantages one can find in the natural desert—which always has variety—or in the ordinary forest, where things grow because the birds bring the seeds and they flourish. I greatly believe, therefore, in the development of true and not imitative garden personality. We gardeners visit indiscriminately and as widely as we can manage, seeing many things.

HE ANSWER to this query is a suitable one for an American to make. There are native roses throughout the North Temperate Zone, according to scientific statement. As a matter of cold, hard fact, the rose was, as I see it, intended by God to benefit all the world before it was first exploited in the easily habitable world. If I delve into the information gathered during a lifetime, I discover that many hundreds of years before Christ there were roses in the habitable world, and that they were loved most heartily. In that portion of world history that includes the formation of the Athenian and Roman empires, roses were known and grown. There are even depressing stories of royal women who virtually bathed in rose petals, with the raising of which they had nothing to do.

Right now we may say that all the world has roses, and can have more of them. It happens that after quite a period of relatively slow renewal of the rose impulse, there now comes a time when rose plants are not only desirable, but are in very short supply. It is not in point here to argue the reason for this; the fact is that rose plants are hard to come at, and are high in price when they are obtainable.

There arises then the question of relative desirability. Anyone who browses as I must do to keep myself happy, finds that our English and French friends had roses even by the thousands of varieties more than a century ago. Paul's wonderful book, published in the London neighborhood in 1848, describes intimately more rose varieties than I ever hope to see. In due time the process of improvement, resting upon personality plus God as usual, flowered in a great Frenchman, M. Pernet-Ducher. In his little nursery near Lyons he made the great changes which resulted in most of the roses grown today. He brought into the current rose stream the brilliant colors one now sees in the best bright red roses. These had previously appeared in commercial varieties and until then broadly speaking, one grew either Tea roses or Hybrid Perpetual roses. There was also a list of curiously named items none of which had the everblooming quality or the brilliancy we expect nowadays.

This Frenchman, whose letter to me written in 1919 I deeply cherish, really knew roses, as was apparent to a thoughtful American investigator, John C. Wister, when he visited Pernet-Ducher at his home. Mr. Wister found there many surprising roses, and particularly noted the way in which this great hybridist had fenced off the bees from hybridizing by nature's method. M. Pernet-Ducher, it seems, wrapped the blooms he had fertilized with "little twisted papers on the rose stems."

Few other hybridizers have used the extreme care which in the hands of this rose genius gave the world a new kind of rose. (I must not be misunderstood. Hybrid Teas had been made before the introduction by Pernet-Ducher of his brilliant and rich colors. But they really started from these efforts.) Again personality entered, because these things occurred right on the edge of the first World

Souvenir de Claudius Pernet Rose, a living memorial to the second son of M. Pernet-Ducher, its originator. This and the Georges Pernet have been dispersed widely over the world

Few rose hybridizers have had a magic touch superior to that of M. Pernet-Ducher, who crowned his achievements with this
SOUVENIR DE GEORGES PERNET ROSE

War and this Frenchman had sent two sons to the front, both of whom were killed. It is their memorials that live for the world as Souvenir de Claudius Pernet and Souvenir de Georges Pernet.

Now these good roses, produced not only in France but also in England and in America, were exchanged through the ordinary processes of friendship and commerce. They did not stay on the European continent nor remain in America, and they soon disregarded the scientific formula as to the South Temperate Zone by becoming very useful and popular in Australia and New Zealand.

So the question comes to be asked about what the point of origination of a rose plant has to do with its future life. For many years we in America did not grow our own roses, bringing them very largely from the nurseries in Germany, Belgium and France, and, with much less vigor, from England. They were mostly "budded roses," which I cannot at this time attempt to distinguish in detail, and the understock used was an Italian sort which received the name of Manetti. The time came when America could not be con-

tented with importing roses, cheap as they
were because they were grown by the ill-paid
labor of Europe. Our own ingenuity turned
us toward other understocks and we have had
many millions of roses grown on various of
these, principally the Japanese Multiflora, or
on what is really the wild rose of England,
Rosa canina.

Meanwhile rose producers have covered
the country pretty well, because a good nurseryman likes to grow roses. In addition to the
central vigorous and high-producing territory
within a two-hundred-mile radius of the national capital at Washington, the Pacific
Coast has produced many roses. They have
been grown freely in Georgia and Florida,
and much more freely in Texas, so that quite
throughout the country rose production has
continued and commercial rose interchange
has occurred. In my experience the point of
origin has nothing whatever to do with the
prosperity a rose plant will attain in one's
own garden, provided it is carefully planted
and treated with reasonable decency. I well
remember the feeling I had when in 1927 a
considerable number of roses produced in

Australia, and largely grown by another wiz-
ard of the rose, Alister Clark of Victoria,
came to Breeze Hill.

This was after a series of quarantine inves-
tigations, discoveries and conclusions had
involved a trip to Washington to untangle. I
did not know whether these roses would prosper. They had left Australia several months
previously at the end of the growing season,
so that they were dormant according to the
standards we use in America. Somehow, if
there is a consciousness in rose wood, it was
borne in upon that consciousness that the
long trip from the other side of the world was
the same as a long winter, and every one of
the roses grew off with vigor and complete
rose propriety. In fact, I still cherish some of
those original plants. (I had taken the pre-
caution to divide my shipment with a good
rose man living in Chevy Chase, one of
the outskirts of Washington, who I thought
would have certain advantages of location.
His plants grew also, just as well as mine did.)

Many times I have planted roses from the
far Pacific Northwest, and, if they were at all
good rose plants, they grew. Many times as

well I have planted even more roses grown in the great state of Texas. The eastern portion of that state has a climate peculiarly favorable to the rose family; at least the Texas nurserymen look at it that way. The result was always the same, provided the start was right. Later experiences showed that from time to time ambitious growers would jump the game, so to speak, by shipping roses before the chill of winter had defoliated them, performing the act by a curious and not commendable process of sweating off the leaves. The plants would arrive quite good-looking, but they did not grow that way, and in one notable case where I selected a small block in East Texas, had it defoliated by all the methods known, and shipped to Breeze Hill, the result was a complete failure. We had interrupted the course of nature too sharply.

Now all I have written here about roses and where they come from, as well as where they get to, refers to the major supply of Hybrid Tea and Hybrid Perpetual roses that are propagated by the budding method. This method has almost entirely supplanted the old grafting practice. This was a winter inside operation of quite considerable efficiency, offering, however, no real advantages. I cannot recommend to anyone who reads these words a more interesting garden experiment than to do a little budding for himself—or probably herself. All that is required is young growing shoots of any rose, of whatever parentage it might be, and a live bud from another rose which it is desired to propagate. With a sharp knife slit a section of the first-named rapidly growing rose for about an inch and a half, and then make a little cross-cut so that, with a skillfully handled knife blade, the bark can be lifted. The new variety, represented by a single bud that has been cut from the stem, can be readily slipped under this moist and encouraging larger stem and should then be tied into place, usually with a rubber band or a piece of raffia. If this budding is properly conducted there is an actual union between the bud and the stock on which it has been inserted, and after a little time the growth beyond the place of the incision can be cut away so that the whole of the vigor of the root will be put into the new growth. (This is quite awkwardly said, I know, but most people who read it will have seen budding so that it will be a familiar operation.)

Now all of this propagation by budding, covering some hundreds of millions of roses every year, is virtually new compared with the old process of rose propagation through cuttings. By that method, as conducted in the greenhouse, a young shoot was cut off the desired variety and rooted in sand, just like a cutting of a geranium or any other familiar house plant. If it did root it could then go into the open and become a good rose under favorable conditions. There were once tremendous propagations in America by this method, but as there was no outdoor opportunity in the process, these little plants had a hard row to hoe, and many of them didn't hoe it.

It is fitting to say here that a great many roses of the stronger growing hardy kinds are successfully grown from cuttings. This includes all of the species sorts and most of the climbers, and all that is necessary is to know who does the work to be assured that one is not wasting time in planting the result.

As a matter of everyday garden fact, it is

much better not to do budding personally, but to buy roses from a reliable firm with a reputation to sustain and a record of accomplishment.

I hope I have made it plain that the point of origin has nothing to do with the future of the rose plant under discussion, provided it has been permitted to mature normally so that the foliage was removed from it by frost, and has been treated as a living thing until it gets into your garden. There it should receive not only your attention but your love, which is an essential part of the growing mechanism.

$\mathcal{S}$HAKESPEARE said, "A rose by any other name would smell as sweet." Without arguing the question, I doubt it. At any rate there is but one name for that flower which dominates the world—the rose. It has been my great privilege recently to see rose fossils millions of years old, proving clearly that what we now know as a rose was a rose in the long ago, even before the time of cave men.

But the plant that is worrying me just now —if a good blooming plant can really worry me—is one we call easily the mockorange (it isn't orange and it doesn't mock anything) or "syringa," (it isn't a syringa and doesn't imitate a syringa.) We have to get down finally to the scientific name, *Philadelphus,* and when I think of the blank stare that clouds people's faces when we use that term, I realize that the plant is virtually unknown by its true name. Thus it is that misunderstanding surrounds one of the most desirable plants of eastern America as it blooms in May-time gardens.

Philadelphus grandiflorus, commonly known as "Mockorange,"
or Philadelphus, occupied a large part in Dr. McFarland's heart
as well as in his Breeze Hill garden

In the days before I was obsessed with the Breeze Hill desire I did know *Philadelphus coronarius,* the common mockorange, than which just one is sweeter. There is a larger variety, *P. grandiflorus,* which spreads its flowers widely but which has none of the rich fragrance of the genus. The name seems to have been attached hundreds of years ago because somebody wanted to compliment the Egyptian king Ptolemy Philadelphus. He did his job about 280 years B. C.

Other and very distinct blooms and still more distinct fragrances followed as the sixteen species established at Breeze Hill grew to blooming height. It early appeared that the French hybridizer to whom we owe so much, Victor Lemoine, had done all sort of things with the Philadelphus family. He seemed to have the habit of utilizing one exceptionally sweet-smelling sort to transmit his magic. This *P. microphyllus,* which came from the Utah, Colorado, Northern Mexico and California region was distinct in form and notable in fragrance. That greatest of plant encouragers, Charles Sprague Sargent of the Arnold Arboretum, seems to have been Lemoine's source for the species. He crossed it in many directions building up a series of extremely notable and attractive varieties. Some of these, as I have said, varied in form and style. One of them (Belle Etoile) has a refined purple dot at the one petal's base, and leaning forward to prolong sensory enjoyment one inhales a fragrance of something very like gardenia.

Because it was easy and handy, there grew up one variety called Virginal, slightly double in its petalage, and generally of the same fine style characteristic of the genus. The French hybridist was in no trouble about getting attractive names. He had Atlas, Avalanche, Bouquet Rose (with no rose in it), Candelabra, Conquete, and the distinct Girandole, to say nothing of Glacier and my own rather difficult fragrant pet, Belle Etoile.

I don't have any idea of blaming the nurseryman if he mixes these mockoranges. One couldn't conveniently get a bad one in the lot, and the man who takes his garden seriously enough to appreciate and compare his blooming luck will find no difficulty whatever in believing that the Philadelphus or the mockorange or the syringa, or all of them, are tremendously useful shrubs.

In the passage of years one sees these great plants develop sometimes to eight feet or more in height. At Breeze Hill we have our own idea as to pruning, so that each season we cut out the older stems and some of the abundant number of shoots that spring up about the plant. There is only one thing that the gardener must keep in mind, and this is that if he prunes in the spring he is cutting off that year's blooms. It is obviously best to prune the mockoranges *after* they have bloomed.

Both America and Asia have contributed basic varieties to this superb genus. It isn't as plentiful as the lilac, which is the true Syringa—and it is encouraging to find that the name authority, "Standardized Plant Names," calls the lilacs Syringa, as they are, and keeps the Philadelphus as mockorange (without a hyphen).

I don't know which of the American nurserymen has the largest list of Philadelphus varieties. Checking up my own sources of information, I discover that I have got them from all over the map. It seems that I was always willing to take a Philadelphus from anyone who was sure to have it honestly named. In this connection I feel like urging that those who read what I write will also remain convinced as to the right name of this plant. It is easily verifiable if there is a public library nearby in which can be found Bailey's "Cyclopedia of Horticulture" or "Standardized Plant Names." We derive so much more pleasure from a plant if we really know what it is and can name it accurately.

It will be noted that I am not insisting on any particular kind of Philadelphus, although my friends won't be really happy unless they have the true mockorange fragrance in the variety *P. coronarius* and the true gardenia fragrance in Belle Etoile. The family is one that provides a hardy and enduring shrub that will flourish in sun or shade (not too much of the latter) and will display a flood of fragrant white bloom when the spring comes back again—right through May and early June.

S̶O RAN the words of a deed given long
ago to the Lutheran congregation of the town
of Manheim in Pennsylvania's rich Lancaster
Valley. From the deed which I have held in
my reverent hands to photograph, I hereby
quote:

> "This Indenture Made the fourth day of De-
> cember in the Year of our Lord One Thou-
> sand Seven Hundred and Seventy two Between
> Henry William Stiegel of the Town of Man-
> heim and Elizabeth Stiegel his Wife of the one
> part and Peter Ereman Henry Wherly and
> Wendell Marzall Trustees and Wardens to
> and for the only use Purpose and Benefit of
> the German Lutheran Congregation settled
> and established in the same place of the other
> part . . . for and in Consideration of the Sum
> of Five Shillings lawful Money of Pennsyl-
> vania . . . All that certain Lot or Piece of
> Ground situate lying and being in the town of
> Manheim . . . said Lot being known in the

AMERICAN BEAUTY ROSE. The rent was paid with one red rose

General Plan of said Town by No. 220. . . . said Peter Ereman, Henry Wherly, and Wendell Marzall and the survivors of them and the Heirs and Assigns of such survivors . . . yielding and paying therefor unto the said Henry William Stiegel His Heirs or Assigns at the said Town of Manheim in the month of June yearly for ever hereafter the Rent of One Red Rose if the same shall be lawfully demanded."

It will be noted that this rent of one red rose was payable only "if the same shall be lawfully demanded." So was recorded the wish of a most picturesque character, who was born in Cologne, Germany, on May 13, 1729, and who reached Philadelphia on August 31, 1750, on the ship *Nancy*. From his later life one can be quite sure that he did not live quietly in Philadelphia, because quietness was not in his make-up. He came to Brickerville in Lancaster County, returned after a time to Philadelphia, and then became established at Elizabeth Furnace. Here Herr Stiegel got far away from the rose, for he became an ironmaster, building up an establishment in which he employed 75 people and made the famous ten-plate stoves that in later years became such treasures and sources of pride to their possessors.

It was as an ironmaster that Stiegel first became famous, although his name comes down to us chiefly as a glass-maker. The few possessors of Stiegel glass bear testimony to the fact that the picturesque German really knew how to produce a marvelously beautiful glass, distinct in its character from any other obtainable then—or since, for that matter— save in imitation.

That church affairs in those days were not conducted as they are now is in evidence as one reads that while Stiegel was living at Elizabeth Furnace or at Brickerville, he help-ed to raise money to sustain the church in which he was so deeply interested through the promotion of a lottery. On the "Twenty-first Sunday after Trinity, 1773," he presented to the church twenty tickets of the lottery he ran that year, stipulating that "if any financial gain came from them the money was to be de-voted to the best interests of the church."

At Elizabeth Furnace, Stiegel established an estate of four hundred acres, to which came to be added several thousand more, pur-

chased from time to time. Within this area
the present town of Manheim was founded by
Stiegel and six others, though he was the actu-
ating spirit. The town was built upon a carefully organized plan which it still in part re-
tains, and represents the first real city planning or "zoning" in Pennsylvania. Here he
erected a mansion for his own residence, with
a platform on the roof where tradition says, a
watchman was stationed to announce the
"baron's" return from any of his various trips
afield. The watchman fired a cannon to greet
Herr Stiegel who always arrived in his coach
and four, with outriders.

Some of this is traditional, but there is no
doubt at all that his employees were expected
to attend the religious services that Stiegel
conducted on Sunday mornings.

Seemingly Stiegel derived much profit
from the Revolutionary War. His foundry at
Elizabeth Furnace ran full blast to provide
munitions for the fighting patriots. But it was
his work with glass rather than with shot and
shell and ten-plate stoves that made him famous. In the Pennsylvania *Journal and
Weekly Advertiser* of July 5, 1770, Stiegel

tells about his "American Glass Ware" in an announcement here quoted:

AMERICAN GLASS WARE

consisting of a very necessary useful and curious variety of white and blue Flint, manufactured at Manheim Glass Works, in Lancaster County, Pennsylvania, to be sold by Brooks and Sharp, at the house of Nicholas Brooks in Front Street near Lombard Street, Philadelphia, where merchants for exportation, retailers in Philadelphia, country storekeepers &c may be supplied with any quantity for cash or short credit, and where all orders from the country &c shall be punctually complied with.

As the proprietors have been at an immense expense in erecting said works, and engaging some of the most ingenious artists in said manufacture, which is now arrived at great perfection, and above all, as at this crisis it is the indispensable duty, as well as interest of every real wisher of America, to promote and encourage manufactures among ourselves, they hope from the glorious spirit of patriotism at present voluntarily and virtuously existing here, to receive the approbation and encouragement of the public, which they expect to merit a continuance of, by selling their goods on much lower terms, than such imported from Europe are usually sold.

N. B. Those Families who formerly sent orders
to the works, which were not complied with,
may be supplied immediately, by applying as
above.

That Stiegel flourished was evident,
though at all times he seemed unable to keep
out of debt. It was this disposition which
brought his sorrowful downfall, for it was yet
possible in those days for a man to be im-
prisoned for debt, even in free Pennsylvania.
Upon due prosecution, his property was sold,
and in December of 1774 he went to "gaol"
as a debtor.

But his energy and vigor continued even
from the debtor's prison, and on Christmas
Eve of that year Governor John Penn signed
an Enactment of the General Assembly free-
ing him from confinement. Stiegel had made
contact with John Dickinson, one of the
signers of the Declaration of Independence,
and with other friends in Philadelphia who
helped him to get going again, but he had to
leave his residence in Manheim. He looked
to Robert Morris, the famous financier of
Revolutionary fame, for a place of refuge for
his family that would be at once safe from the

British and near to the Continental Congress at York. Indeed the Morris family stayed out of town until Philadelphia was no longer comfortable for the British.

But the picturesque German who came to be called "Baron", though in no way entitled to that distinction, is justly most remembered as before noted for his wonderful glassware. He had begun experimenting with glass-making at Elizabeth Furnace building there a glass works, completed according to accessible records in October, 1765. We read from the entry for November 11th, "This day in the afternoon the glass-makers began to work." At first window panes and bottles were made, and it is not without interest to compare wages of those days with industrial rewards of the present day. Thus a record states: "November 12th—Agreement made this day with Conrad Waltz to attend as Sherer in the Glass House—he is to receive the Value of Three Pounds Ten Shillings a month and to find his own accommodations."

Eventually the business became known as "The American Flint Glass Manufactory," and examples of Stiegel glass were sold all over eastern America. Any and all are precious now as they are discovered.

But all this seems a long, long way from the rent of one red rose "if the same be lawfully demanded" on a day in June. This rent was paid several times to Stiegel in person, and then during the period of his misfortune the church neither offered to pay nor did Steigel "lawfully demand" its payment.

It was in 1877 that a young physician, Dr. J. H. Sieling, came to Brickerville fresh from college. Interested in all Pennsylvania history, he promptly became engrossed in the Stiegel legend as previously little-known historical data was unearthed in his neighborhood. He practiced among the farm folk of that rich country, and doubtless thus became inspired with a desire to do honor to the "Baron" Stiegel, of whom older men he met delighted to reminisce. He was told of Stiegel's ambitious undertakings and of the pomp with which he surrounded himself.

Dr. Sieling removed to Manheim, and there lived in the midst of Stiegel memorials. He heard of the exquisite glass that Stiegel had made; of the sermons that the "baron" was wont to preach to his workmen. He ran into the story of the band of musicians said to have been stationed on the roof of the mansion house to celebrate occasions with melody. It was quite in point that one of the older men, a member of Zion Lutheran Church, should tell him the story of Stiegel's relationship to that church, and of the traditional rent payment. Being himself a Lutheran, the doctor hunted up the church records, where he eventually came upon the original deed given the congregation by Stiegel and his wife Elizabeth. The clause in that deed specifying the payment of a ground rent of "one red rose in the month of June, if the same shall be lawfully demanded," stirred him to action.

It happened that a new building was then being erected for Zion Church, and Dr. Sieling suggested that a memorial red rose be placed in the chancel recess, which took the form of a red rose window. Then he planned a church service built around that rent payment of "one red rose." In consequence of his enthusiastic endeavors, the Feast of Roses was inaugurated by Zion Lutheran Church in

1892, and has been continued since then. At first it seemed that no living representative of Stiegel could be found, but one appeared in the person of John C. Stiegel, of Harrisonburg, Virginia. He proved his lineage, and on June 4, 1892, came to Manheim to receive the rent according to the terms of the deed of his ancestor. Through the energetic efforts of the late Rev. J. H. Menges, pastor of the church, other Stiegel descendants were from time to time discovered. Until her death, Mrs. Rebecca Boyer, of Harrisburg, Pennsylvania, a great granddaughter of Stiegel came annually to receive the rent. Her daughters have followed and there has always been a representative to receive "one red rose" on the second Sunday in June. As President Emeritus of the American Rose Society I not only got to know of this ceremony but several times represented the legal heir of "Baron" Stiegel, Mrs. John D. Robertson, when she was unable to accept the rent personally.

In due time a Stiegel memorial boulder and tablet was erected by the Lancaster County Historical Society, and to the annual ceremony came a succession of distinguished men, many of them of Pennsylvania German ancestry. The United States Supreme Court was represented by Justice Owen J. Roberts, who once presented the rose on behalf of the congregation. Most of the Governors of Pennsylvania have been present from time to time at this interesting ceremonial, at which, in addition to the reverent religious services, addresses were delivered that kept alive the memory of Stiegel. (Among other interesting facts, it was discovered that he had been enrolled in the Ninth Battalion Lancaster County Militia.)

Meanwhile Manheim and its neighborhood have been searched for examples of Stiegel glass. Mrs. A. K. Hostetter, of Lancaster, accumulated a notable collection. For some years this Hostetter collection was annually admired by Henry Ford when he came east. He had been told of this evidence of early craftsmanship in the United States and no man loved good work more than he. This is obviously not the place to discuss the qualities of this famous glass, but I can personally testify to the beauty of the specimens I have seen.

This little story of the red rose of Manheim can well conclude with the reprinting
of the last paragraph in a delightful little
book by G. L. Heiges entitled "Henry William Stiegel:"

"As long as Stiegel glass endures and
the Festival of the Red Rose continues
to be celebrated, the memory of Henry
William Stiegel will not perish from the
minds of men."

IN THE First World War there was no active participation by Ethiopia, save a quite incidental relation to the brilliant American-Italian countess whose sons had been lost in air-fighting over that country. After the fighting when the officials of the Department of State and of the Pan American Union were desirous of at least seeming friendly, all the nations of the world were invited to participate in a picturesque ceremony to occur in mid-Africa, the occasion being the coronation as Emperor of Ethiopia rather than as King of Abyssinia of the monarch reputed to be a direct descendant of the Queen of Sheba and King Solomon. There was much conference as to what could be sent from America to properly dignify and celebrate this event. In the course of a discussion between Franklin P. Adams of the Pan American Union and Addison Southard, then the American Minister to Ethiopia, resident in Addis Ababa, it developed that the name of

the capital city signified "The New Flower."
The Minister became quite enthusiastic over
the proposal that a proper remembrance to
this old-world land from the new-world
America might well be a gift of flowers.
There followed a suggestion to the President
of the American Rose Society, who happened
at that time to be myself. There was further
conference with the then Secretary, Robert
Pyle, surely a world rose man if ever there
was one, and we agreed that outstanding
American creations in roses might make a
pleasing coronation gift from the newest na-
tion to one of the oldest.

The difficulties in the transfer of live rose
plants from the Temperate Zone in America
to this African city just under the equator
were long considered. Across the Atlantic
Ocean, through the Mediterranean, the Suez
Canal, and the Red Sea, to little Djibouti in
French Somaliland, whence the narrow-gauge
railroad took three days to reach the 7,800
foot elevation of Addis Ababa—this was the
distance problem we faced. Conference was
undertaken with the officials of the United
States Department of Agriculture (they

would have to permit and prepare the plants for shipment) and the Department of State (to safeguard the shipment between Washington and the Ethiopian capital.) All agreed that it was worth while to make the attempt.

Then came the fine and characteristic American response. In due time 437 good plants of 62 varieties, all of American origin, took the long journey. It became apparent in the correspondence that at this African capital flowers were not only cherished but that they flourished abundantly. Indeed, Addis Ababa was said by the American Minister to have a "really marvelous year-round climate." It had appeared in the discussion that roses bloomed well in this capital city, and that the French, German and Italian embassies all had extensive gardens with plenty of roses. These, of course, were entirely of European origin.

Some twenty nations sent distinguished representatives to the coronation of the Emperor, all bearing gifts, but, as Minister Southard wrote us, "None seems to have created such a deep and favorable impression as this American gift of flowers." In 1931 the Emperor of Ethiopia who had thus been suc-

Haile Selassie's letter of thanks for the "Gift of Roses" sent to
Addis Ababa on his coronation as an expression of good-will
from the American people

cessfully and picturesquely crowned, sent his acknowledgment couched in the official language of his land. This was unknown to any of the officials in Washington and application to the American Bible Society for a translation surprisingly failed to bring the full answer. Then Professor Ralph Marcus of Columbia University discovered that the language was Amharic, and the translated acknowledgment was reproduced in the American Rose Annual for 1932, thus:

The Conquering Lion of Judah
HAILE SELASSIE THE FIRST
The Elect One of God
King of Kings of Ethiopia

May this reach J. H. McFarland, President, American Rose Society.

We extend to you Our thanks for the friendly gesture demonstrated by the tokens of respect which you sent Us in the shape of Roses on the occasion of our Coronation.

(Signed) by the Privy Seal,
SEHAFI TIZAZ WOLDE MESKEL

Later reports indicated that 75 per cent of the plants sent to Ethiopia had flourished. Red Radiance and President Herbert Hoover seemed the best adapted to that genial climate with no winter. There were no troubles reported, because the black-spot and mildew that are the foes of roses in America had apparently not yet reached Ethiopia.

When Italy finally was given credit for capturing Ethiopia, I learned that two sons of one of the American Rose Society's most important European members (the Countess Senni of Rome above mentioned) were aviators of the Italian Expeditionary Force. An attempt was made to find out about the roses, but this failed, and nothing has been heard since as to the present status of the American rose garden in the Ethiopian capital. Possibly now that Ethiopia has been returned to her original monarch, the descendant of King Solomon and the Queen of Sheba may again be cultivating his American roses.

Another geographical celebration of rose supremacy may be reported in the statement that upon the 200th birthday of George Washington the trustees of the American

Rose Society arranged to send 200 roses "born and raised" in America to King Boris of Bulgaria. This came about because an American historian and archivist, Colonel Henry W. Shoemaker, then American minister at Sofia, had found the King and Queen to be very fond of roses. Of course that favorite delaying material, "red tape," interfered, and there was considerable difficulty in getting through the 200 plants that had been so cheerfully furnished by American growers.

But they got through eventually, and the American Minister wrote: "Although Bulgaria observed the Washington Bicentennial in a series of noteworthy commemorations, in no way was it more delightfully observed than by the receipt of the American rose bushes."

The rose bushes were placed in specially prepared beds in full view of the windows of the Queen's apartments. They were well cared for, and probably gladdened the eyes of Bulgarian royalty until the war and the death of King Boris.

HE FIRST two words of this title do not sound "rosy." Long ago the inhabitants of the town near New York's great state prison had its name changed to Ossining, but Sing Sing still gives the sound of punishment to the criminals it houses.

Through the plant hybridist, the late Bertrand H. Farr, attention was first called to letters written by a life convict in Sing Sing that produced an astounding result. And the story of Charles Chapin is hard to tell without tears. Briefly stated, Chapin was a brilliant and successful New York newspaperman, city editor of one of the great papers, with everything to live for, including a talented wife whom he idolized. Just what the turns of fate were that brought him to a suicide pact with her I will not try to tell. The pact was carried out—all but his part— and the wife was dead. He gave himself up to the law with full confession, and was given a life sentence.

At Sing Sing he was quiet, morose, depressed. Something turned him to the healing outdoors, when he could get to it. The lawn space at Sing Sing was limited to a small area in front of the offices, some strips in front of the cell blocks, and one lone flower bed. The Roman Catholic chaplain at Sing Sing, Father Cashin, bought a set of miniature garden tools for Chapin when he was ill, accompanied by the suggestion that a course in digging would not do him any harm! This was merely a jest, intended to stir the prisoner to mental action. It did; he asked if he might be allowed to look after the lawn—a microscopic lawn at that. Then came the search for tools, but there were none. When the first necessities were obtained "the purchase used up a quarter of the budget for the care of the grounds at Sing Sing that year." But there was plenty of time to wait, for Chapin was a "lifer." And when Chapin began to write letters, things began to happen. As he once wrote me, he had available ground in the shape of a crushed

125

rock surface, plenty of labor, a possibility of manure, but no plants and no tools.

Then under the inspiration of that good man, Warden Lewis E. Lawes, things started. Chapin's letters—and he was a brilliant letter writer—brought response from nurserymen. He could get some books, and these he read as he had never read before. He took from the nurserymen whatever they sent and used the donated plants to make a long herbaceous border, planted under conditions in which no borders were ever planted. To quote from one of his friends, Richardson Wright, editor of *House and Garden*, concerning the bulbs:

"These, so they say at Sing Sing, came as a direct answer to prayer. The chaplain was asked to pray for bulbs, and forty-eight hours later a bulb importer on Long Island wrote that he was sending 500, another 1,500, another 2,000, and so on in dizzy succession."

I got into the situation when Chapin told me what he wanted to do about roses. He sent me a plan he had prepared, including some fourteen beds for which he wanted plants. At that time I was visiting many communities and meeting many garden

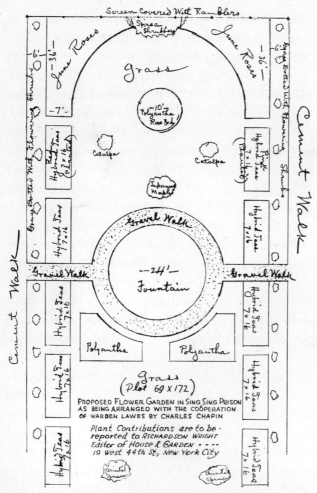

Plan of the Flower Garden which came into being
in the prison yard of Sing Sing

groups, so I told the Chapin story, offering the club or society I was addressing the opportunity to provide plants for one or two of these beds. There was only one trouble about it—most of the organizations wanted to furnish plants for all of them, and one nurseryman really insisted on providing all that was needed. The roses duly came through, and they always flourished. I visited Chapin one time and walked through the rose garden with him, not quite overshadowed by the doleful cell blocks that make up this great prison. For it seemed to me that God through nature gave especial power to the sunshine that reached the surface soil.

On that memorable visit I was deeply stirred by the youth of the prisoners whom I saw during the recreation hour. They were so young, so pitifully young, and so delighted at the sight of the blooms that were then beginning to adorn Chapin's plants. There wasn't any least doubt of the success of the enterprise from the standpoint of its influence on the prison morale. It was reflected in Chapin himself. Warden Lawes wrote:

"In all his active years, even at the pinnacle

of his career, I doubt that he found more spiritual entertainment than in watching the gradual fruition of his ambition—to make a garden spot of Sing Sing's arid patches. He did it with roses . . . It was not a passing fancy with him. The garden became his peculiar province, and the rose, in all its varied hues and tints, his favorite charge."

That the garden as a whole and the rose in particular softened the austerities of Sing Sing I had abundant evidence when one summer day I visited Chapin in company with a great garden woman, Mrs. Helen M. Fox. Admitted as door after door was unlocked, we were in peace and pleasantness when we got into the garden, and to talk and walk with Chapin himself was a deep delight. The warden had permitted the erection of a modest greenhouse, where Chapin in winter time brought beauty out of the ground for the good of all. Proof that he was trusted and loved came when as we emerged into the free open air Chapin called that he had something to give me. He was permitted to come through the doors and hand me a paper, shaking my hand in farewell. I am sure I never shall appreciate freedom as much as I did just at that moment!

The rest of this story is not so pleasant. A change in the drainage system made it necessary to cut across the rose garden with the steam-shovel, and poor Chapin withered with the roses. As Warden Lawes said: "Chapin looked sorrowfully at this carnage, but he was helpless. His province was being laid waste. I think it affected him deeply. He was never the same afterward. He was suddenly the helpless invalid, unable to carry on. Shortly thereafter he died." The Warden continued:

"Chapin's province is being reconstructed. The rose hedges will again stand guard at its borders. They will be living, conscious realties, breathing of the spirit and soul of their godfather, Charles Chapin—Sing Sing's Rose Man."

From the other side of the country comes another story of the effect of roses on prison morale. One February this note arrived from W. A. Bridwell, of Forestburg, Texas: "Dear Mr. McFarland: A gardener and flower lover who is in prison at San Quentin, California, wants a copy of the Rose Annual. If you have

one, please mail it to John Martin, Box
37388, San Quentin, California."

This not only moved the Annual of that
year promptly toward San Quentin, but
brought a response from the prisoner himself
that began a correspondence running over
several years. At least one visit was made to
see John Martin by a California member of
the American Rose Society. In the course of
the correspondence it became apparent that
the prisoner was a real plant lover, and that
the authorities were quite willing to provide
him with a parole under certain conditions,
one of which was that he be assured employment before he left the penitentiary. This
proved quite difficult, and was itself the basis
of much correspondence.

But Martin's response to me was immedi-
ate, for he received the first copy of the American Rose Annual in warm gratitude; after
the acquaintance had developed he wrote:
"Perhaps you do not realize the help it brings
one who has been to the bottom of life and is
engaged in the difficult task of climbing back
to worthwhile levels. The task is not an easy
one." It was possible to bring him into con-

tact with some plant people in California who could and did give attention, but they could not produce immediately the employment that was a condition of his release. There were times when he was completely discouraged, and when it seemed necessary to stir his ambition. At no time did he fail to say that his greatest hope was to handle plants. He described in detail "The Garden Beautiful." Inquiry in other directions developed that this was a place in the prison where electric light continually shone and where some plants flourished. His descriptions of the roses that bloomed under continuous electric light were most interesting. He seemed to be an expert plantsman and to have had opportunity to develop beauty inside the penitentiary.

To me the correspondence was most moving, despite the fact that sometimes Mr. Martin found the road hard to travel and was discouraged. He did eventually find employment. The last letter concerning him arrived one day and read thus:

"On Christmas day John Martin went to the rescue of a woman when a car was careening toward her in a safety zone. He saved her, but was injured himself, never coming out of the brain concussion which followed, though he lingered for some two weeks . . . . His crime was against woman, and he went out in a blaze of glory, wiping clean the slate."

That flower-growing or horticulture of any sort has great penological value has been proved to me not only through the two instances here cited, but through other evidence. I visited a certain penal institution in New York one rose season, but there was not a rose inside the dour and dreadful gates. Nor was there a smile or the hint of a smile on the faces of the painfully young prisoners. Another experience took me to a correctional institution for boys, with an approach much like Sing Sing's. My errand on that visit was to tell a rose story in pictures to eight hundred boys legally confined. These unfortunates were intensely interested, and showed the interest by audible questions among each other. This caused the warden to give them a sharp reproof and the whole spirit of the thing was immediately destroyed. When I escaped from that place I felt that there was no mitigating value possible in the surroundings.

Then came a time when I visited a similar institution for women, conducted by a humane and extraordinarily able woman warden. She had several hundred women of all ages and conditions, including some "lifers." There was no fence about the place, no bars or locks were in sight, and segregation only was used for punishment, rarely at that. To these women of all ages I showed the pictures I had presented to the boys not many weeks previously. The response was vastly different, and as I went about the great farm that was cultivated by these women prisoners I found proof that growing things have much to do with mental rehabilitation. And I always had the same feeling of pleasure that so much help could be given so simply, and indeed so profitably—if one is mean enough to look at the cost—by the sight of growing crops, roses, and other flowers.

134

THE ROSE MAN OF BREEZE HILL

by Robert Rodale

HE BEST FRIEND of the rose in America, J. Horace McFarland, died at his home in Harrisburg on the second of October, 1948. He was 89 years old.

Whenever we hear of an individual who scoffs at man's normal life span and advances into his eighties and nineties we feel open admiration for him. He has seen and absorbed much of life and has observed the passing of many eras. He can be compared to the wise owl, sitting on his perch and watching the activity of the world, knowing all. If he is of the caliber of J. Horace McFarland, he has no remorse.

Dr. McFarland (he received his degree of Doctor of Humane Letters from Dickinson College) had no patent formula for his longevity. Perhaps it was his devotion to his work, his interest in life, and his desire to live that kept him alive and alert. The fact that he

136

never smoked or drank might enter into the picture.

Dr. McFarland was a man of manifold achievements. Besides being a connoisseur and capable judge of roses and plants in general, he was a master printer. Infected with the printer's ink germ as a boy, he remained in that profession until his death. Only the finest work in color and monotone was allowed to leave his plant.

He continuously sought to preserve the natural beauty of our national parks and to beautify American cities. The American Rose Society was his pet. His desire to publicize the rose and arouse interest in this queen of flowers led him to build the organization to its present size.

A native of his favorite state, Pennsylvania, Dr. McFarland was born in McAlisterville, Juniata County, September 24, 1859. His father moved the family to Harrisburg in 1865. In 1871, when John Horace was 12, Col. McFarland took two steps that were to have great influence on his son: He abandoned teaching as a profession and went into the nursery business. A short time later, he started a temperance newspaper. That combination of interests, printing and horticulture, was to stick with Dr. McFarland until his death.

At the age of 19, he opened a small print shop in his own name, and eleven years later purchased the old school building that was the nucleus of the present plant, known as the Mount Pleasant Press. The firm name, J. Horace McFarland Company, was adopted in 1891, seven years after his marriage to Lydia S. Walters. They had two children, a daughter, Helen, and a son, Robert, who now manages the press.

Dr. McFarland was never satisfied with anything less than the best in printing, horticulture, city planning, or any of his other fields of endeavor. When he began printing seed catalogs, an item that now makes up 95% of the output of the Mount Pleasant Press, he realized that the woodcuts then in use did not graphically represent the plants. Dr. McFarland felt the need of a better medium of illustration, and the infant science of photography seemed to be the answer. Experienced photographers were scarce in those days, so he had to do much of the early work himself. In fact he is credited with originating several photographic formulae. Today, the Mount Pleasant Press has in its files one of the world's largest assortments of horticultural photographs.

Black-and-white photography soon lost its appeal for Dr. McFarland, who felt that the true beauty of nature could never be reproduced without natural color. Consequently, he spent the year 1894 in New York managing the Coloritype Company, introducers of a German-invented three-color printing process still largely in use today. His experience with this company enabled him to do color printing of the highest quality in his Harrisburg plant.

Although the first actual color photographs produced on this continent are believed to have been made at the Mount Pleasant Press in 1907, Dr. McFarland was never satisfied with the variable results obtainable by direct color photography. He always felt that the only accurate way to reproduce the colors of nature was to have an artist superimpose them on a black-and-white print. Nearly all the color printing done by his company today involves the use of hand-colored photographs.

Dr. McFarland spent a tremendous amount of time growing, testing, publicizing, photographing, and writing about his favorite flower, the rose. However, he never did any breeding of new types of roses. In the fall of 1915 he visited the famous Elizabeth Park rose garden in Hartford, Conn., and immediately realized the potentialities of municipal rose gardens. It was his desire to spread the cultivation of this outstanding flower among the people of the United States—along the roads, about the homes, and in the parks.

It was in 1916 that Dr. McFarland became affiliated with the American Rose Society, of which he was president from 1930 to 1932 and in which he remained a prominent figure. He edited and published the "American Rose Annual" and the *American Rose Magazine,* organs of the rose society, from 1916 to 1943. Seeking to publicize the rose, he scoured the world for information on new types of roses being developed. He established a method of rose identification and registration for use in the "Annual". Although interested in all phases of rose growing, Dr. McFarland always favored amateur rose growers and the outdoor rose growers who catered to amateurs rather than the hot-house growers and florists.

One of Dr. McFarland's customs was to conduct a rose service at Grace Methodist Church, Harrisburg, every June. He provided and dedicated cut roses which flower girls distributed to the congregation.

Dr. McFarland was often asked by the many visitors to Breeze Hill to name his favorite rose. He usually named the rose he happened to be holding in his hand at the time. However, he occasionally admitted a preference for three blooms named in his honor, "The Doctor", the "Editor McFarland," and the "Horace McFarland."

One of Dr. McFarland's first efforts in the fields of horticulture and printing was the *American Gardening Magazine,* which he printed and contributed to from 1901 to 1903. Besides editing twenty-eight "Annuals" of the American Rose Society, Dr. McFarland wrote a number of books on horticulture subjects: "Roses of the World in Color",

141

"Photographing Flowers and Trees", "Getting Acquainted with Trees", "Laying Out the Home Grounds", "My Growing Garden", and "The Rose in America", co-authored "How to Grow Roses", "Garden Bulbs in Color", and "What Every Rose Grower Should Know". He also edited the "Beautiful America" department of the *Ladies' Home Journal* from 1904 to 1907.

Motivated by his love of nature and her unregimented beauty, Dr. McFarland continuously fought to preserve and develop our National Park areas. He was instrumental in having Yellowstone turned into a National Park and was appointed to the first National Park Board by President Wilson. The need for protection of Niagara Falls was also realized by Dr. McFarland. Seeking to determine who actually owned the falls, he worked for the treaty with Great Britain and was appointed as the American representative to the Niagara Control Board by President Coolidge. Evidence of the quality of his leadership on these boards is the fact that, although a Republican, he kept his appointments during Democratic administrations.

Ardent exponent of city planning and beautification that he was, in 1904 Dr. Mc-Farland went to St. Louis to assist in the formation of the American Civic Association and became its president. The city of Harrisburg, his residence for all but a short period of his life, received his special attention. It is now a bustling and beautiful city with many parks and well laid out streets. Dr. McFarland traveled over the entire country praising Pennsylvania's capital and telling "the Harrisburg story". He was always campaigning for roadside betterment and the elimination of highway billboards, and gave freely of his time to other public works as well, becoming active in a number of local and national societies.

On six occasions he was awarded a gold medal in recognition of outstanding service—two in 1933; by the American Rose Society "for his unstinted effort for the advancement of the rose in America," and by the Massachusetts Horticultural Society (the George Robert White Medal of Honor) for "eminent service in horticulture". The American Scenic and Historic Preservation Society gave him the Cornelius Amory Pugsley gold medal in 1938. The inscription described him as a "leader in the protection of Niagara Falls, in establishment of the National Park System, and in general city and park betterment, especially in Harrisburg, Pa." Dr. McFarland's service to nature, plants, and flowers was recognized in 1939 when he was awarded the Arthur Hoyt Scott Garden and Horticulture Award. For his "distinguished service in the realm of the rose" he was given the Jane Righter medal by the Garden Club of America, and the Dean Hole Memorial Medal by the National Rose Society of England, both in 1942.

With the death of J. Horace McFarland a great leader was lost—not only in the fields of horticulture and printing, but in society as a whole. His efforts to make this country a more beautiful and pleasant one in which to live affected millions of people from many localities. A man of high ideals, his goal in life was to spread happiness and joy. The world will not soon forget the rose man of Breeze Hill.

144